21st Century Skills **INNOVATION** *Library*

Snowboarding

by Jim Fitzpatrick

INNOVATION IN SPORTS

Published in the United States of America by Cherry Lake Publishing
Ann Arbor, Michigan
www.cherrylakepublishing.com

Content Adviser: Thomas Sawyer, EdD, Professor of Recreation and Sport Management, Indiana
State University

Design: The Design Lab

Photo Credits: Cover and page 3, ©Eric Limon, used under license from Shutterstock, Inc.; page 4,
©iStockphoto.com/Silvrshootr; page 5, ©JJJ, used under license from Shutterstock, Inc.; page 6,
©iStockphoto.com/ParkerDeen; page 9, ©iStockphoto.com/piskunov; page 10, ©iStockphoto.
com/Sportstock; page 11, ©iStockphoto.com/dlewis33; page 13, ©iStockphoto.com/ArtBoyMB;
page 14, ©iStockphoto.com/Caval; page 17, ©iStockphoto.com/SAMIphoto; page 19,
©iStockphoto.com/Julijah; page 20, ©iStockphoto.com/MarcoCoda; page 21, ©iStockphoto.
com/Jeya; page 23, ©Buzz Pictures/Alamy; page 24, Courtesy of Scott Starr; page 25, ©AP
Photo/Alden Pellett; page 27, ©AP Photo/Todd Bissonette; page 28, ©Ronald Karpilo/Alamy

Library of Congress Cataloging-in-Publication Data
Fitzpatrick, Jim, 1948–
Snowboarding / by Jim Fitzpatrick.
    p. cm.–(Innovation in sports)
Includes bibliographical references and index.
ISBN-13: 978-1-60279-260-9
ISBN-10: 1-60279-260-7
1. Snowboarding–Juvenile literature. 2. Snowboarding–Technological
innovations–Juvenile literature. I. Title. II. Series.
GV857.S57F59 2009
796.939–dc22   2008007554

Cherry Lake Publishing would like to acknowledge the work of
The Partnership for 21st Century Skills.
Please visit www.21stcenturyskills.org for more information.

CONTENTS

CHAPTER ONE

Birth of a New Board Sport

Snowboarding is a fun but physically demanding sport.

Snowboarding is a wonderful way to enjoy a winter's day. Snow-covered mountains invite snowboarders of all ages to carve turns as they ride to the bottom of the slopes.

What's amazing is that snowboarding began with surfers who rode the waves in the warm ocean waters of Hawaii, California, and Florida. When the surf was "flat" (when there were no waves), they wanted to have

Surfers and snowboarders stand in a similar way on their boards.

fun onshore. So a few innovative surfers began to make skateboards to ride on streets and sidewalks. A whole new sport became popular—skateboarding! At that time, skateboarding was almost like surfing, and at first it was called sidewalk surfing. Standing on their boards—on a wave or on a sidewalk—surfers and skateboarders felt the same excitement.

Some of those same innovative surfers and skateboarders wanted to keep having fun during the winter. Another new sport—snowboarding—was born. By experimenting and trying out different ideas, surfers and skateboarders soon discovered they could enjoy standing on their boards and carving turns down snow-covered slopes.

Many snowboarders love the winter season—and snow.

Early snowboards were very simple and not too safe. One of the first versions of a snowboard was invented in the 1960s. It was Sherman Poppen's "Snurfer," a combination of a wooden sled and a skateboard deck. It had a rope attached to the front, which the rider held on to. And it had steel tacks in the surface that helped hold the rider's feet in place. In the 1970s, surfer Dimitrije Milovich teamed up with surfboard maker Wayne Stovekin. They developed another version of a snowboard. It was based on a surfboard design with metal edges. Milovich went on to found the Winterstick brand of snowboards.

As they developed better snowboards, early snowboarders discovered another problem. Unlike the ocean for surfing, or sidewalks for skateboarding, there were not many public places to snowboard. Skiers and snowboarders both need snow-covered mountains. The mountains also need to have open trails without trees and boulders in the middle. Most ski areas in the United States are privately owned. When snowboarders first arrived at many of the resorts, they discovered they weren't welcome. Most ski resorts told snowboarders they couldn't use their slopes.Snowboarding was banned!

Even though they weren't allowed to use the slopes at most ski areas, early snowboarders kept improving their snowboards, boots, and other equipment. They kept

Learning & Innovation Skills

Snowboarding sometimes seems to have a language all its own. One snowboarder might say to another, "Dude, you pulled that air to fakie right into an alley-oop on the other wall. That was so rad!"

Do you and your friends have your own special terms in the hobbies or sports you pursue? Have you ever created your own words?

trying to find places to practice and get better at the sport they were inventing. Often they would have to climb or walk to the top of mountains or hills. They would then strap on their boards and ride them down the slopes. Instead of riding a chairlift back up the mountain like a skier would, they would walk back up to the top for another run. For some, the challenges made snowboarding more interesting.

Today, there are millions of snowboarders around the world. With the development of safer equipment, snowboarders were eventually able to show skiers they could enjoy ski slopes together. Now most ski areas encourage snowboarders to ride alongside skiers on the slopes. There are even winter sport areas that are designed especially for snowboarders.

CHAPTER TWO

Creating the Rules

Rules for sports often result from safety concerns. Or they evolve because the game being played requires the team or the players to do certain things. One example is the rule in baseball that if a batter gets three strikes, the batter is out. Then the next batter gets a turn to try and hit the ball. When a baseball team gets three outs, it's then

Good snowboarders are courteous. They give other boarders time and space to enjoy the slopes.

the other team's turn to try to score runs. Snowboarding, like surfing and skateboarding, doesn't have rules like those in other sports. Surfing doesn't have rules about which surfer can ride a certain wave. There are no rules for which direction a skateboarder should ride.

Snowboarding is different, too, because the only runs are those you take when you ride down the mountain slope. A run in snowboarding is everything a snowboarder does from the top of the slope to the bottom. The turns, the jumps, and the tricks are all considered part of the run.

During a run, many muscles work to help a snowboarder stay balanced and change direction.

Maintaining a safe distance allows snowboarders to avoid collisions if someone falls.

Even though there isn't a rule book for snowboarding, snowboarders have developed their own "code." The code allows people to snowboard with others in a respectful way. Even though the code is unwritten, most snowboarders seem to understand the importance of following these guidelines for everyone's safety.

One of the basic parts of the snowboarder's code is the same as that for skiers. When riding down the mountain, it is the responsibility of the snowboarders higher on the slope to avoid getting too close to or

Learning & Innovation Skills

 Professional and amateur snowboard competitions are the only events where snowboarding rules exist. In fact, success in competitions sometimes comes from one competitor knowing the rules better than another. Snowboard competitions often include time limits. Most slalom or downhill competitions are races against the clock. Those who can complete the course in the least amount of time are the winners.

The Winter Olympics, Winter X Games, and U.S. Open Snowboarding Championships are now broadcast worldwide. So millions of people only know snowboarding as a competitor's sport. Most snowboarders, however, have never been in competitions. Their interest is more about enjoying themselves while learning tricks and improving their skills.

Do you think champion snowboarders still enjoy trying new moves and tricks?

colliding with those below them. It's easier to look down the slope and adjust turns and direction than it is to look up the slope.

Another part of the code applies to snowboarders and skiers in snow parks or terrain parks. These are areas where boarders and skiers construct bumps, ledges, and even a **half-pipe** for use. In snow parks, it is very important to take turns. It's also very important to pay attention to the direction of other skiers or boarders and to not **snake** other riders.

CHAPTER THREE

Innovations in Equipment

The three Bs of snowboard equipment are the most important: board, **bindings**, and boots. Also very important are a good safety-approved helmet and the right type of layered clothing.

Snowboards have developed over time into safer boards. They are usually made of layers of wood, plastics, and **composite**

Goggles protect a snowboarder's eyes from the wind and sun.

materials. The materials are compressed into different sizes and shapes. Snowboards are now made for riders of all sizes and ability. When he was younger, Olympic champion Shaun White had to use adult-

Snowboards are lighter than they used to be. This makes it easier for snowboarders to carry them around the slopes.

sized snowboards because no one made small boards for younger snowboarders. More people are beginning to choose snowboarding as their favorite way to enjoy snow-covered slopes. So today's snowboards come in a range of sizes and **flexibility**.

In the early days of snowboarding, one piece of equipment hadn't been invented yet: bindings that attached the snowboarder's boots to the boards. Most early snowboarders wore hiking boots or ski boots when they attempted to stand on their makeshift snowboards. When they lost their balance, it usually meant they lost their snowboard, too. The boards would continue down the mountain without their owners. It's easy to imagine how dangerous that was for other skiers or snowboarders farther down the slope! A snowboard rushing down a mountain without anyone to control it could cause serious injury to anyone it hit. Unfortunately, this happened enough times that many ski areas banned snowboarding. The owners thought that snowboards were too dangerous.

To solve this problem, snowboarders developed new types of boots and bindings. They allow movement while also providing flexibility with the board. Another addition to the bindings and boots was the type of safety strap that many skiers have. The safety strap connects the bindings to the snowboarder's leg. That way, when a

21st Century Content

 Innovative snowboard manufacturers continue to create new products and materials. As the sport evolves, their product lines evolve to meet the needs of snowboarders. Today, there are even snowboards that turn into skis at the flip of a small latch. Known as a splitboard, this snowboard can split down the middle into two skis! This means that a snowboarder can ski up a slope in the style of a cross-country skier. Then, when ready, he can secure the latch and ride down the slope on the converted snowboard!

snowboarder falls, if the bindings open and release the board, the strap will keep the board from taking off down the mountain.

An approved helmet is a really important piece of safety equipment for all snowboarders. As with many other sports, there are dangers when snowboarding. Most snowboarding injuries are minor sprains and strains to ankles, knees, and wrists. These types of injuries often heal quickly. Head injuries, however, are much more serious. So it is important for all beginning snowboarders to wear helmets to protect their heads.

Another important safety concern is the correct type of clothing. Most snowboarding takes place outside in very cold conditions. Snowboarders usually wear several layers of clothing so they can adjust to changes in temperature during the day. Weather conditions can change quickly in the mountains. Waterproof and windproof outer layers, such as a hooded jacket and pants, are best. Layers of wool, silk, or microfiber worn underneath help snowboarders remain comfortable as the weather warms or cools. Innovative clothing manufacturers are producing jackets, pants, and other items that are perfect for cold snowboarding days.

Believe it or not, snowboarders can get sunburned, so it's important to use sunscreen.

Innovations in Learning and Technique

Snowboarding, like surfing and skateboarding, has much to do with balance. Unlike those other sports, a snowboarder's feet are attached to the board. It can be a challenge for beginning snowboarders to keep their balance. If you start to lose your balance while doing most other activities, you can move your feet to keep yourself from falling over. When you are snowboarding, however, your feet are attached to your board. You can't move them to stop yourself from falling. Snowboarders have to develop new kinds of skills to keep from falling.

Getting on a board is the first step. It's important to know which of your feet will be your forward foot when you stand on your board. If your left foot is forward, that position is known as regular. If your right foot is forward, that means you are **goofy-foot**. You can find out for

Beginner snowboarders should expect several falls before getting the hang of the sport.

yourself whether you are goofy or not, with the help of a friend or relative. Stand comfortably with someone behind you. Have that person, without telling you, give you a gentle shove from the back that is strong enough to force you to catch your balance by moving your feet.

If you put out your left foot to steady yourself, that means you're regular. If you used your right foot, you're goofy.

Pioneering snowboarders began with a few simple skills. Then they developed more advanced tricks and maneuvers that emerged from the basics. Basic turns are an important skill because there are no brakes on a snowboard. Snowboarders must learn how to make **frontside** and **backside** turns so they can stop

Performing jumps takes a lot of practice.

Some tricks are dangerous. Only experienced snowboarders should try them.

themselves. Once a boarder's forward foot is in the binding, the boarder will be able to use his free foot to push himself along in the snow. This action is similar to skateboarding. Gliding on the board (with both feet in the bindings) is an early skill. Then comes traversing, which is riding crossways to the fall line (the easiest path down the slope).

Over the years, many enthusiastic snowboarders have invented new tricks and maneuvers. Some of those,

Learning & Innovation Skills

 The ollie is the basis for many snowboarding tricks. Once it is mastered, other, more complicated tricks are possible. The ollie was first done by skateboarder Alan Gelfand, and it completely changed skateboarding. Can you figure out why a snowboarding ollie is easier than one on a skateboard?

Unlike skateboards, snowboards are connected to the snowboarder's feet! By bending the knees and reaching up with the arms, all while jumping up, a snowboarder can quickly learn to ollie. Then, when the ollie is mastered, it's time for an alley-oop. A boarder ollies into the air and, while still in the air, reaches down and grabs the board while rotating a half-circle. That's it—an alley-oop!

like the **ollie**, were inspired by skateboarding or other sports.

Today's snowboarders don't have to worry about where to practice and master new tricks. As more people took up snowboarding, snow park owners saw an opportunity. Accomplished snowboarders can now practice their sport at several winter areas devoted especially to snowboarding. Many snow parks feature embankments, stairs and railings, and half-pipes. They also offer long twisting slopes and steep runs. There are even indoor snowboard parks in Europe and Asia where snowboarders can enjoy their sport year-round!

CHAPTER FIVE

Some Snowboarding Innovators

Snowboarding is still new compared to many other sports. Innovative snowboarders are the ones pushing the limits to come up with new tricks and gear. Here are a few of the people who have helped to make snowboarding so popular.

The sport of snowboarding keeps evolving. Snowboarders work hard to come up with challenging and exciting moves.

ACTION NOW

$2.00

DECEMBER 1981
VOL. 8, NO. 5

SNOWBOARDING:
Is this the year?

U.S. PRO SURFING CHAMPIONSHIPS

In 1981, Tom Sims appeared on the first magazine cover to feature snowboarding.

Tom Sims

In 1963, while at Haddonfield (New Jersey) Middle School, Tom Sims created a "skiboard." It was an early version of the snowboard. Unfortunately, he never patented his invention, so whether he was the first inventor of the snowboard is still up for debate. He went on to be a snowboard champion. He was also a snowboard stunt double for Roger Moore (James Bond) in the 1985 movie *A View to a Kill.* The Sims Snowboard brand is now part of a bigger company, but Sims remains involved with the business.

Jake Burton Carpenter

The innovative snowboard designs of the 1970s
and 1980s were largely influenced by Jake Burton
Carpenter. Born in New York City in 1954, he founded
Burton Snowboards. His products cover every aspect of
snowboarding: snowboards, boots, bindings, and clothing.
In addition, the company put together a team of world-
class snowboarders.

Jake Burton Carpenter began his company in 1977.
Today, it is a leader in the snowboarding industry.

Lindsey Jacobellis

As a 15-year-old, Lindsey Jacobellis entered her first Winter X Games in the boardercross. This is a head-to-head contest against four other snowboarders. Participants race down slopes while snowboarding over and above jumps and turns and gaps. Born in Danbury, Connecticut, in 1985, she first began snowboarding with her older brother, Ben. He was a snowboard champion. She also competes in half-pipe competitions, but it is her participation in boardercross races that has brought her so much fame. After winning four gold medals at the Winter X Games, Jacobellis was the favorite to win the Olympic boardercross gold medal in 2006. But while in the lead and only three seconds from the finish line, she fell and had to settle for the second-place silver medal. The following year, during the 2007 Winter X Games boardercross race, she again fell while in the lead. But at the 2008 Winter X Games, the determined Jacobellis would not be denied. She raced to the first-place gold medal once again.

Shaun White

In men's snowboarding competitions, the "10" has defined for many years who would be crowned champion. First developed by Ross Powers and Danny Kass, the "10" is the snowboarder term for an **aerial** trick with

Lindsey Jacobellis is an inspiration for other women who dream of excelling in the sport.

3 complete rotations (1,080 degrees, or a "10-80").
Many believe it was Shaun White's ability to complete
a 10 during his first run that clinched the 2006 Winter
Olympics gold medal in the half-pipe competition. Born

Not only is Shaun White a great snowboarder, but
he is a talented skateboarder, too.

in Carlsbad, California, in 1986, White began winning amateur and then professional competitions as a teenager. He didn't stop with the 10-80. He has continued to push himself to reach new levels of achievement. During the 2008 Winter X Games, he won the gold medal with a run that included a "12-60." That's three-and-a-half rotations (1,260 degrees). Will the 12-60 become known as a "12," to match up with the 10? The trick is still so new that snowboarders aren't certain. But most agree on one thing: it makes them dizzy to even consider trying it!

Glossary

aerial (AYR-ee-uhl) describing tricks done off the ground

air to fakie (AYR TO FAY-kee) a move that involves riding up the wall of the half-pipe, ollieing from the lip (edge), and then (without changing direction) riding back down the half-pipe wall to the opposite side; your forward foot becomes your back foot, and your back foot the front, so in a sense you're "faking" the direction you're going in

alley-oop (AL-lee-OOP) a move that involves riding up the half-pipe wall, ollieing from the lip, then (while airborne) rotating your body and board a half circle and landing on the half-pipe wall with your same forward foot still forward; also called "ollie-oop"

backside (BAK-side) types of turns with your back toward the mountain; sometimes called heelside

bindings (BINE-dingz) straps that attach a snowboard to a snowboarder's boots

composite (kuhm-PAH-zit) made up of two or more distinct substances

flexibility (flek-suh-BIHL-uh-tee) the state of being able to move, bend, or adjust

frontside (FRUHNT-syde) types of turns with your body facing the slope; sometimes called toeside

goofy-foot (GOO-fee-FOOT) a term for riding with your right foot forward, whether on a snowboard, skateboard, or surfboard; this term comes from surfing when, in the early 1960s, most surfers in California rode with their left foot forward; if you had your right foot forward, you were considered "goofy"

half-pipe (HAF-PIPE) a U-shaped structure with opposing walls, used for snowboarding tricks

ollie (AH-lee) a move in which a snowboarder transfers weight from the front foot to the back foot to snap the board up off the ground

rad (RAD) awesome or cool

slalom (SLAH-luhm) a kind of race in which competitors run a course through a series of gates to test technique, speed, and agility

snake (SNAYK) to cut quickly in the path of another skier or snowboarder

For More Information

BOOKS

Gifford, Clive. *Snowboarding*. New York: DK Children, 2006.

Hughes, Morgan. *Snowboarding*. Vero Beach, FL: Rourke Publishing, 2004.

Slade, Suszanne. *Let's Go Snowboarding*. New York: PowerKids Press, 2007.

Weinstein, Anna. *Kevin Jones: Snowboarding Superstar*. New York: Rosen Publishing Group, 2004.

WEB SITES

ABC of Snowboarding
www.abc-of-snowboarding.com
Learn about snowboarding history, get tips, and read about current news

United States Ski and Snowboard Association
www.ussa.org
For information about this group, which oversees clubs and competitions throughout the country

U.S. Snowboarding Team
www.ussnowboarding.com
Meet the members of the current U.S. team

Index

About the Author

Jim Fitzpatrick has been involved with board sports since 1957. He was a long-time skateboarder and surfer by the time he first snowboarded in the 1980s. "It was a disaster!" he claims. Since then, he has become an accomplished snowboarder, and now he can't decide which board sport he enjoys the most. A California native, Jim lives in Santa Barbara and Sausalito, California. Founder of the Santa Barbara Montessori School, he is now head of Marin Montessori School, and is busy developing a junior high school curriculum that will include winter snowboarding trips to nearby Lake Tahoe's slopes.

WITHDRAWN